THE VIC CRIMINAL

Neil R. Storey

SHIRE PUBLICATIONS

Published in Great Britain in 2011 by Shire Publications
Ltd, Midland House, West Way, Botley, Oxford OX2 0PH,
United Kingdom.

44-02 23rd Street, Suite 219, Long Island City, NY 11101,
USA.

E-mail: shire@shirebooks.co.uk   www.shirebooks.co.uk

A CIP catalogue record for this book is available from the
British Library.

Shire Library no. 615.   ISBN-13: 978 0 74780 814 5

Neil R. Storey has asserted his right under the Copyright,
Designs and Patents Act, 1988, to be identified as the
author of this book.

Designed by Tony Truscott Designs, Sussex, UK
and typeset in Perpetua and Gill Sans.
Printed in China through Worldprint Ltd.

09 10 11 12 13   10 9 8 7 6 5 4 3 2 1

COVER IMAGE

Frederick Losh Mills (sixty), manager of the *Army and Navy
Gazette*, pleaded guilty to falsifying a cash book and
embezzling monies to the value of £1,900 from his
employer and was sentenced to four years' penal
servitude. John Bennett (thirty-eight), boot finisher, was
convicted of wounding with intent Annie Owen, the
woman he lived with, and received five years' penal
servitude.

TITLE PAGE IMAGE

The criminal and the long arm of the law as pictured in
Illustrated London News.

CONTENTS PAGE IMAGE

A pair of Victorian police handcuffs.

ACKNOWLEDGEMENTS

I am grateful for the help and support of many people in
the production of this book. In particular I would like to
express my gratitude to: my friend and fellow crime
historian Stewart P. Evans; Robert Bell of the Wisbech and
Fenland Museum; the Galleries of Justice, Nottingham;
Lincoln Castle Prison Museum; Hugh Alexander at the
National Archives; Norfolk Library and Information
Service; Gordon Taylor, Archivist at the Salvation Army
International Heritage Centre; Helen Tovey at *Family Tree*
magazine; Essex Police Museum; Norfolk Police Archive;
Thames Valley Police Museum; University of East Anglia
Library; Dr Stephen Cherry; the late John Mason; James
Nice; Nick Wright and Russell Butcher at Shire
Publications; and of course my loving family.

Most of the illustrations and images are taken from
originals in the author's archive. Permission to use images
has been sought; any omissions are unintentional. Other
images, as indicated, are published by kind permission of
Stewart P. Evans, the Wisbech and Fenland Museum,
Thames Valley Police Museum, Mary Evans Picture Library
and the National Archives.

Illustrations are acknowledged as follows:

Mary Evans Picture Library, pages 32, 35 and 37;
Stewart P. Evans Archive, pages 14, 16 (bottom right), 44
(bottom left), 53 (bottom) and 58; The National Archives,
pages 54 (top) and 57; Thames Valley Police Museum, page
31 (bottom); Wisbech and Fenland Museum, pages 11 (all)
and 36 (top).

Shire Publications is supporting the Woodland Trust, the UK's leading woodland conservation charity, by funding the dedication of trees.

CONTENTS

INTRODUCTION

DURING THE REIGN of Queen Victoria (1837–1901) many old laws were reviewed, penal reform continued and the first organised modern police force in the world was created, but crime and criminality remained a constant. The types of offences changed, reflecting a changing society with increased industrialisation and growing urbanisation, while age-old motives continued to generate crimes born out of desperation, unemployment, poverty and hunger. It was also an unprecedented time for the opportunist thief, because, as society became increasingly affluent, more homes, businesses and individuals presented targets and temptations for the criminally inclined. As ever, there were still those crimes that are the result of the frailties of human nature, such as rage, jealousy, avarice and hate. Indeed, it can be said that the nineteenth century was punctuated by some of the most dramatic and horrible crimes of modern times, reported in lurid detail even in the respectable national and provincial newspapers, while the gutter press such as the *Illustrated Police News* was flagrant in its graphic depictions and reportage of the most violent and horrifying crimes.

The new police were frequently criticised for their failure to catch the perpetrators of crimes, especially the high-profile cases that hit the national press. Their situation was not helped when members of the Detective Branch were exposed in a corruption scandal in 1877 that led to the complete reorganisation of the branch into the new Criminal Investigation Department (CID).

In the 1870s forensic science was still in its infancy; some poisons could be detected but it was still difficult to prove scientifically the difference between mammalian and human blood that may have been found on the clothes of a suspect. Crime scene investigation was variable; in many cases the priority seemed to be the removal of the body to the mortuary rather than the detailed examination of the scene intact. In the absence of anything else more convincing, the pseudoscience of phrenology, the study of the shape and features of the human cranium, was popularised in the first half of the nineteenth century, culminating in the 'advanced' theories expounded

Opposite: Viewing the death masks of murderers executed at Newgate, from *Illustrated London News*, 1873.

Some prisoners were less than co-operative when being photographed.

by Cesare Lombroso and Alphonse Bertillion, whose system of anthropometry, based on measurements of the physiognomy of convicted criminals, was adopted by British and American police forces and prisons in an attempt to establish a formula to identify the typical 'criminal type'.

When Scotland Yard's Fingerprint Bureau was established in 1901 and the first conviction based on fingerprint evidence, that of the brothers Alfred and Albert Stratton for the Deptford Cash Box Murders, was secured in 1905, the Bertillion system was made redundant.

No matter how efficient the police were, if there were no witnesses or the locals were unco-operative, and if there were few clues to work on, detective work in the nineteenth century was often extremely challenging.

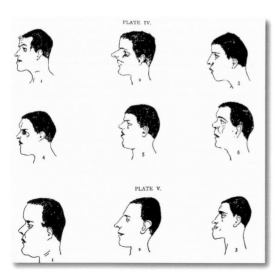

PLATE IV.

PLATE V.

Studies of the physiognomy of the 'criminal type'.

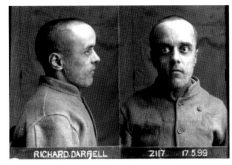

Above: Albert George had been behaving in a disorderly way in St John's Road, Holloway, on 4 October 1896, and when PC Haynes intervened George brutally attacked him. George pleaded guilty to unlawful wounding, and was sentenced to three years' penal servitude.

Above: Richard Darrell, labourer, was a member of a dangerous gang of letter-box thieves. Brought before the County of London Sessions in 1899, he was found guilty of stealing a cheque for £5 5s from a pillar box on the Edgware Road. He was sentenced to three years' penal servitude.

Below: The Crime Museum, also known as the 'Black Museum', of crime relics at Scotland Yard was formerly open by appointment to members of the public. Although it is now closed to the public, fascination with crimes of the nineteenth century remains undiminished.

THE RURAL CRIMINAL

W HEN QUEEN VICTORIA ascended the throne in 1837 parish lock-ups and stocks were still being maintained and used. The use of lock-ups is understandable in the days before adequate police transport or a 'modern' police force, as we would recognise it, when the unpaid parish constable needed to detain drunken or violent individuals until they had sobered up or cooled down, before they were brought before the magistrates. The stocks dated from medieval times and were the oldest and most widely used punitive device still in use for the punishment of minor offenders during the nineteenth century. For the country magistrate and the prison system as a whole, the use of parish stocks saved time and money. A person brought before the bench and found guilty of minor offences such as drunk and disorderly behaviour could thus serve his or her sentence without the involvement of prison admission, paperwork, government issue clothing or food. The punishment would involve the miscreant being locked in the stocks for a few hours in the space of a day. By the 1850s the use of the stocks was petering out, and the last recorded use was at Rugby in 1865.

Analysis of any rural county's statistics of crime in the nineteenth century reveals that the most common offences brought before the magistrates included trespass, vagrancy and breaches of the Poor Law, but two crimes above all absorbed the majority of the magistrate's time – theft and offences against the Game Laws. Thefts in rural areas tended to be very petty in nature, such as stealing food, items of clothing or small amounts of money; these offences usually attracted short custodial sentences, ranging from about a week to three months. County gaol books tend to be filled with columns stating the offence as 'stealing'. Persistent offenders might also face transportation, until its abolition in 1868.

Highway robbery was still a frequent occurrence well into the nineteenth century. Despite the romance attached to Dick Turpin and his fellow 'gentlemen of the road', highway robbery, typically aimed at solitary travellers, often on horseback, has always been violent, terrifying and

Opposite:
A violent exchange by moonlight between poachers and gamekeepers, as depicted in *The Illustrated London News*.

potentially fatal. Under the cloak of shadow or darkness small gangs of highway robbers would set upon their victim; one or two men would grab the bridle of the horse while other gang members (some of whom were occasionally women) assaulted the rider, often striking a blow to his head or face, then dragging him off the horse to the ground. The victim would be beaten unconscious, after which his clothes and panniers would be rifled for anything of value. Highway robbery was a capital offence until the 1830s, when the death penalty was replaced by transportation or penal servitude with hard labour.

Landowners had fought an often losing battle against poachers of 'fur, feather or fin' for generations. The 1722 'Black Act' had been the response to troublesome instances of deer

Above: A good example of a village lock-up, erected in 1838 at Needingworth in Cambridgeshire.

Right: Stocks were maintained by law in every village, town and city parish across England. This example, with a willing participant, was photographed in the early twentieth century at Cranworth in Norfolk.

Far left: Charlotte Bird (twenty-nine), a domestic servant, convicted of stealing two pots of jam and a handful of other comestibles in April 1875, was sent to Wisbech Prison for fourteen days with hard labour.

Left: Robert Ambrose (fifty-three) of Outwell, sent to Wisbech Prison for one month with hard labour in October 1873 for wood theft.

poaching, in particular a poaching gang known as the Wokingham Blacks. This robust law made it a capital offence to hunt, wound or steal deer, rabbits, hares or fish in the King's forests, to break down the heads of fishponds, or simply to go about armed and disguised anywhere that game was kept. Landowners also employed man traps and spring guns to deter poachers, but despite all these deterrents poaching continued. The Black Act was repealed and spring guns and man traps were outlawed for use outdoors in 1827. However, their use was still permissible in houses between sunset and sunrise as a defence against burglars.

James Hunt (forty-one), pictured in 1873, had served a sentence for highway robbery in 1851, for which he was transported for ten years. Upon his return, he carried on as a thief and served further sentences at Wisbech Prison.

Poaching remained a criminal offence after the repeal of the Black Act. Indeed, it became far more prevalent and was soon regarded as one of the fastest growing crimes in Britain; in some rural counties as many as one in four convictions was for offences against the Game Laws. Poaching carried progressively harsh sentences for repeat offenders. Very few

The classic *I Walked by Night*, first published in 1935, was written by Fred Rolfe under the sobriquet of 'The Life of the King of the Poachers' and edited by Lilias Rider Haggard.

THE LIFE OF THE KING OF POACHERS

I Walked by Night

Edited by
LILIAS RIDER
HAGGARD

Illustrated by
EDWARD
SEAGO

poachers would come quietly if they were disturbed by the gamekeeper during their nightly vigils, and murderous and extremely violent exchanges pepper the court records and provincial newspapers throughout the nineteenth century.

Times were hard and those who found work on the land often had to endure periods of unemployment, when they would find it difficult to feed their often large families, living hand to mouth from day to day. Therefore the local poachers were often well known and appreciated for the cheap meat they could supply to villagers, who would usually protect their identity from enquiries by gamekeepers or constables. With so many country people in the same situation, many men owned a shotgun and most men and boys knew how to set a snare to catch a rabbit and

A gin trap for rabbits: such devices, along with wire snares, were stock-in-trade for country poachers during the nineteenth century.

would occasionally resort to a bit of poaching to keep their family fed. However, there would often be one or two men in a village who regularly went poaching. They would be the ones who knew the land well, and perhaps they were the more colourful characters who found it difficult to hold down employment but achieved a certain mystique and even a folk hero status by standing up to foremen, employers and local authorities, and received the sympathy of many local people if they were caught poaching and sent to prison. Unlike arson, highway robbery and cattle, horse and sheep stealing, which all declined in the latter half of the nineteenth century, poaching remained a common feature of rural life.

Top: Gamekeepers and brushers on the Ketteringham Hall Estate, Norfolk, c. 1900.

Right: Notorious Norfolk poacher and prison breaker Robert Large was in trouble with the police in 1906.

NORWICH CITY POLICE.

Photo and description of

ROBERT LARGE,

alias "Seymour," an ex-convict and notorious poacher, wanted on warrant in this City, charged with assault on Police on 13th August, 1904.

Aged 37 years, height 6 feet 1 inch, swarthy complexion, dark brown hair, brown moustache, brown eyes, proportionate build, stoops slightly, long, swinging gait; a native of Gt. Witchingham, Norfolk. Marks:—scar middle forehead, left side neck, scar front left thumb, palm of hand, back little finger, top joint left little finger contracted, scar inside and outside front right wrist, scar right of back and front left shin, mole left shoulder.

Dressed usually in light brown coat and vest, cord trousers, cap, and heavy lace boots.

May be found associating with poachers and thieves, or at low Public-houses.

Please cause every possible enquiry to be made for this man, and if found, arrest and wire me, when an officer shall be sent for him, or any information obtained kindly communicate to

E. F. WINCH,
Chief Constable.

The Guildhall, Norwich,
24th August, 1904.

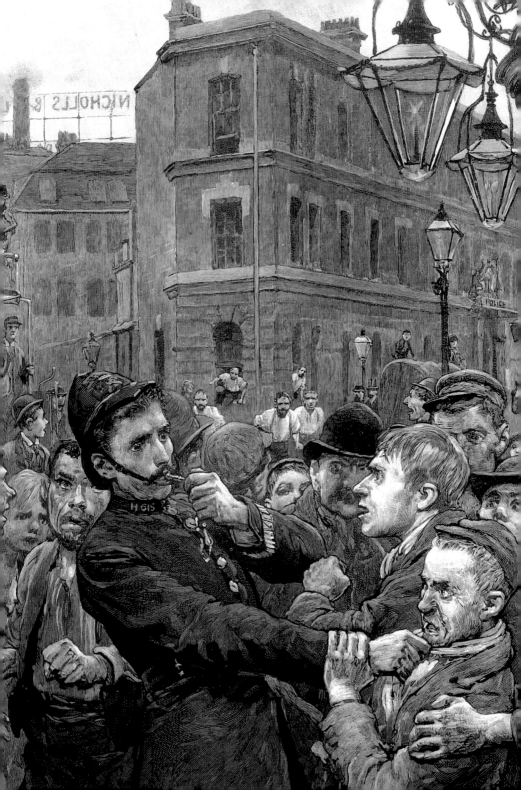

THE URBAN CRIMINAL

THE CRIMINALITY of urban areas shares some common features with rural crime, such as drunkenness, disorderly behaviour, petty theft and domestic violence. Some crimes, however, were far more prevalent in cities, where 'white collar' crimes such as embezzlement, fraud and forgery could flourish. There were also instances of riot and terrorism, notably the 'Fenian Outrages' in the 1860s and 1880s. Urban courts saw far more cases of theft than their rural counterparts. Indeed London and other urban court records show that almost 80 per cent of cases brought before them during the nineteenth century involved an act of theft. There were far more opportunities for burglary and theft in the large towns and cities, to the extent that some criminals acted as full-time 'fences', who disposed of stolen goods on the black market.

If the breadwinner was laid off from his or her regular work, even in the burgeoning cities of the nineteenth century, a family could rapidly decline into poverty. Once a household had pawned or sold all it could to survive, and if poor relief failed to support them, many would turn to stealing rather than be reduced to entry into the workhouse. The items stolen would often be food, or sometimes pitiful amounts of money to buy food, and there were seasonal trends: firewood, for example, was a popular target during long and cold winters. Those driven to steal from properties through desperation often did so by crude means of breaking and entering, but with a more advanced industrial society came cheap and effective tools for the more skilful burglar. Many of these criminals had served apprenticeships or laboured in a trade such as carpentry or building, and found that their skills could be used in the illegal but lucrative sideline of burglary. A range of burglary equipment more akin to a craftsman's tools would include a brace and bit with various blades and drills, a gimlet, chisels and hammer, with additions such as an 'outsider' (fine pliers with modified jaws for grasping the butt-end of a key in a lock), devices for cutting or extracting wooden panels and glass panes, jemmy, skeleton keys or 'picklocks', crowbar, rope, dark lantern and collapsible ladder.

Opposite:
The situation looks ominous as a crowd gathers around a miscreant, and the constable blows his whistle to summon assistance on Commercial Street, Whitechapel, London, c. 1889.

Domestic violence was tragically an all too common feature of both rural and urban life in the nineteenth century.

Below right: A set of burglars' pick-locks and skeleton keys.

Below: A Bradford Borough Police wanted person notice from March 1894.

County Borough of Bradford.

POLICE NOTICE!

£2 REWARD.

Escaped from Custody at 10·30 p.m., on 17th inst.

JAMES HOLLAND, alias Gillespie, Labourer, age 25, height 5 feet 7 inches, brown hair, brown eyes, brown moustache, stiffish build. Distinctive marks:-.C.G. and Bracelet right arm; several other marks on left arm. Dress:—Old black worsted coat and vest turning brown, pair of Police Uniform trousers, and peaked cap.

The above reward will be paid to any person giving such information as will lead to his arrest. Information to

JAMES WITHERS, Chief Constable,
OR
A. W. DOBSON,
Chief Inspector Detective Department
Central Police Station, Town Hall,
BRADFORD, March 19th, 1894.

The most infamous of all Victorian burglars was Charles Peace. An habitual criminal, he was also a skilled musician, but his violin case was often used to carry his burglary equipment. Between 1851 and 1872 he spent a total of sixteen years in prison. In 1876 Peace turned from burglar to murderer when he shot PC Nicholas Cock during a robbery at Whalley Range, Manchester. He also shot his ex-lover's husband, Alfred Dyson, at Banner Cross as Dyson attempted to intervene when Peace accosted the woman. Peace fled but was finally captured in the act of burgling a house in Blackheath in October 1878. Tried and sentenced for this crime under one of his aliases, John Thompson, Peace was recognised at Pentonville

Charles 'Charlie' Peace, burglar, murderer and bogeyman of the late nineteenth century.

A 'penny dreadful' artist's impression of Charles Peace's desperate bid to escape from the moving train transporting him to Leeds to stand trial for murder in 1879.

The enduring interest in Peace saw chapbooks and broadsides about him printed long after his execution.

Prison by one of his former warders and was soon despatched by train to Leeds to face trial for the Banner Cross murder. During this journey Peace made one last attempt to escape and flung himself out of the train window. The train was brought to a halt and Peace was discovered unconscious, having landed on his head. Found guilty at Leeds Assizes, and with all hope of a reprieve gone, Peace confessed to the murder of PC Cock and was hanged at Armley Gaol on 25 February 1879. Peace became a bogey figure, the subject of many broadsides and 'penny dreadfuls'; even years after his execution mothers would warn naughty children: 'Don't do that or Peace will get you.'

Another urban criminal was the 'coiner', typically a man too old to work the streets, or perhaps a skilled jeweller turned to dishonesty. The coiner would usually be found operating from a garret room in a city tenement, where he would set about making plaster casts of coins of the realm, mostly the silver ones such as crowns, half-crowns and florins. When these were prepared, he would stoke up a coke fire in his grate, over which he would hang a melting pot filled with base metal, which, once molten, he would ladle into the moulds to cast his forged coins. When they had cooled down, he would 'finish' the coins by filing off traces of the cast, and would then use a simple battery-operated electro-plating device to 'silver' the coins.

When they were ready to enter circulation, the coiner would pass his forged coins to his 'snide pitcher', who would buy the coins at half face value, or share the profits with his 'smasher', who would attempt to pass the coins as genuine and obtain goods for resale, or buy some small item, receiving the change in genuine coins.

Letter-box thieves, or 'fishers', were an urban criminal type operating in the more affluent areas of cities, where people might send money, valuables or indiscreet letters (ideal for selling on to blackmailers) by post. Noting the times a street pillar box was emptied by the postman, the thief would be able to judge when the box would be filling up. When the coast was clear, the thief would 'fish' for letters by means of a line with a lead weight attached to the end, which would be smeared with birdlime to stick to the letters and allow them to be pulled out when the line was hauled up.

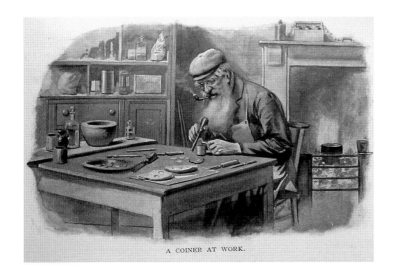

A COINER AT WORK.

A coiner going about his work, as depicted in *Living London* by George R. Sims (1901–3).

The 'sharper' operated on busy city streets, especially near stations, where gullible visitors might pass. He would often locate himself near an alleyway or on a street where he would have more than one way to make a swift exit. Many sharpers would employ a look-out to watch for suitable 'marks' (gullible people to be lured to the scam) or policemen. More than merely three-card tricksters, sharpers worked a variety of scams such as the 'ring dupe', in which the innocent passer-by was induced to buy an item such as a worthless ring or a musical instrument from the sharper, who claimed it to be of great value and told a sad story that he had fallen on hard times and was forced to sell the treasured item but had neither time nor inclination to find a better market. There was the 'painted bird trick', whereby a worthless sparrow was painted or coloured and passed off as a valuable canary or piping bullfinch, deceiving many ladies. There were even 'fly' horse dealers, who would, by artful means, make worthless horses appear valuable. The sale of the animal being necessitated by the death of a relative, every promise was given of a fair trial and return of the money if it was not satisfactory; of course, all promises and paperwork were later found to be worthless.

Forged coins cast in base metals: good and poor examples of the coiner's art.

The 'swell mobsman' was a confidence trickster who affected a smart appearance and adopted a sham foreign title or rank to convince boarding-house keepers in respectable areas of cities to accept bogus cheques, or to defraud shops of goods supplied on credit or sent on approval. Others, similarly attired, worked the main railway stations of major cities and towns.

Stepping out from a first-class carriage, with an authoritative air they would summon the nearest porter and get him to hail a hansom cab, claiming they were late for an appointment or needed to catch a connection at another station. In the throng of the alighting passengers, the trickster would point out 'his' luggage to the porter, stating that it had his printed luggage labels on it. They would be loaded on the carriage and he was off. Only later did it emerge that he had slapped his labels on someone else's luggage while the porter was hailing the cab.

Visitors, especially those from the country, would often be warned by friends of such dangers before they went to the city. Cautions were even published in guidebooks such as Dickens's *Dictionary of London* (1879), where readers were warned:

> Among the many thieves who infest the London streets none are more artful
> or more active than carriage thieves. No vehicle should ever be left with
> open windows and valuable rugs in victorias should always be secured to the
> carriage by a strap... Ladies should be especially careful of officious persons
> volunteering to open or close carriage doors. In nine cases out of ten these
> men and boys are expert pickpockets.

Others operated in pairs, targeting four-wheeled cabs with their roofs laden with luggage and parcels. Running behind the carriage, one thief would clamber up the back and lift off one of the parcels, unbeknown to the driver, and pass it to his accomplice, who was running behind. Once it was safely off, the two would run in different directions and meet later at an agreed place to divide the spoils.

The female pickpocket: one false arm in her muff leaves the real one free to reach through a discrete open seam in her cloak to rifle her neighbour's handbag for valuables.

Female pickpockets were far more sophisticated, better dressed and successful than the common street 'dipper'. Using a series of false compartments in her voluminous skirts, false arms and hands masked by gloves and muffs, the pickpocket would keep her real hands free inside her clothes to dip out from a side panel to pick the pockets of those sitting beside her on an omnibus or tramcar. Well-to-do gentlemen were a popular target for another scam. A girl would 'mistakenly' greet the man as her uncle, placing her arms around him; her 'error' would be corrected in a mannered

A variety of nefarious and distractive acts by female pickpockets are depicted in this magazine feature from the early 1880s.

way but, as the man straightened himself and strode off he might well find that his wallet and watch-chain were missing, and the girl had disappeared among the crowd.

For those who walked the less salubrious streets of big cities there were darker dangers. In the mid-nineteenth century London was gripped by a garrotting scare. The garrotter was sometimes a male criminal, but more often a female felon, who had a better chance of getting closer to her victims, by posing as a prostitute. When the target was taken into a dark alley and suitably vulnerable, either the 'prostitute' would punch him hard in the throat or an accomplice would come from behind with a scarf or similar ligature, quickly flip it round the victim's neck and with a rapid jerk render him temporarily insensible, while the woman robbed him of his wallet and watch-chain. This means of robbery became so feared that leather anti-garrotte neck stocks were sold and *Punch* satirised the crime:

The old 'Stand and deliver's' all rot
Three to one; hit behind; with a wipe round the jowl, boys,
That's the ticket, and *Vive la Garrotte*.

A female garrotting gang in action, *c.* 1875.

If the victim remained insensible on the ground, there were always 'mutchers' about who would 'skin the stiff', rifling the body for anything else of value, even clothing and boots.

'Snuffer gangs' operated in pubs in the lowest areas of cities, especially near docks, where they would prey on newly paid-off seamen. After buying a sailor a drink, they would surreptitiously add some 'brown powder' to it. If the unsuspecting sailor downed the draft, he would soon be stupefied and hustled from the bar to get some air. Bundled down some dark alley, his hands tied or held, he would then be severely beaten and robbed. If after this 'doing over' he still looked capable of raising the alarm, the gangs

would not think twice about throwing their victim headlong into the river, from where his body would be recovered a few days later, and another appeal for the identification of a nameless body would grace the police notices.

Before the 1880s dens of iniquity, to suit all classes, were to be found in every city. In 1857 *The Lancet* estimated that one house in every sixty in London was a brothel, and one woman in sixteen a prostitute. If this is to be believed, it meant there were six thousand brothels and eighty thousand

A snuffer gang and their unfortunate victim, *c.* 1880.

A pocket revolver with foldaway trigger, otherwise known as a 'life preserver', a popular defence against footpads for the man about town in the mid-nineteenth century.

Mabel Gray, whose real name was Annie King, began as a shop girl in Regent Street but rose to become an infamous London demi-mondaine and high-society prostitute in the 1860s and 1870s.

Elizabeth 'Lizzie' Lock, East End 'unfortunate' and petty thief, shortly after admission to prison in 1897.

prostitutes in London in the mid-nineteenth century.

The Criminal Law Amendment Act (1885) caused the closure of many brothels and it also enacted that two prostitutes must not share a rented room to live and sleep. Punishments for lodging-house keepers were stiff but women were often able to take clients back to rooms if they were discreet. However, many more prostitutes than ever took to conducting their business in the shadows off the streets. Following a number of increasingly serious assaults on these vulnerable women, 'pimps', otherwise known as 'ponces' or 'bullies', saw their chance to claim their 'dues' (protection money) from the prostitutes working in their territory, lest 'something terrible' should happen to them.

As many as one in eight women in the East End of London saw prostitution as their main source of income; the percentage was considerably higher if one included the women who occasionally turned to 'the oldest trade' when on hard times. Prostitutes were of all ages; some, working in their forties and fifties, were described as 'painted and haggard', but in 1888, when the age of consent was thirteen, the Salvation Army was giving refuge to girls aged between eleven and twelve; some were as young as ten.

There were distinct types of street-walkers. The youngest, prettiest girls, who commanded the highest prices, were found in the West End; the finest were in Mayfair, followed closely by those in Soho and Piccadilly. The 'nice girls' were to be found around Hyde Park, Bayswater, Victoria and Maida Vale; the 'cheaper girls' were found around Euston and King's Cross, and, finally, when most were too old, too diseased, too drunk or 'too unfortunate', they could end up as an 'East End Floosie'. Prices varied, too: guineas might be be lavished on the West End girls, whereas the street women of the East End saw half a crown to ten shillings as 'good going'. Most of the older women would be happy with the price of a night in a doss house or a glass of gin (about 3d), or even a loaf of stale bread, for their services.

W. T. Stead, the editor of the *Pall Mall Gazette*, exposed white slavery in Britain in the interests of investigative journalism. In 1885, with the help of Josephine Butler and acting at all times under the proprietorial supervision of Bramwell Booth of the Salvation Army, Stead found Rebecca Jarrett, a reformed prostitute and brothel-keeper. With Jarrett's help Stead 'bought' a thirteen-year-old virgin named Eliza Armstrong from her alcoholic mother for £5. Stead published the story as a series of sensational articles in the *Pall Mall Gazette* as the 'Maiden Tribute of Modern Babylon'. The story exposed a disgusting trade and caused outrage across the nation. Soon Parliament was discussing what was to be done about this abominable business. Despite all propriety being shown and Miss Armstrong being untouched, the act of procurement and charges of abduction brought by the girl's father (his permission had not been asked) landed Stead and some of his associates in court. Booth was given a stern warning by the judge but he and a number of others were acquitted, while four others, including Stead, were sent to prison. Stead was sentenced to three months. He was first sent to Coldbath Fields Prison, then to Holloway as a first-class inmate for the rest of his sentence. Stead would later reflect on his days in what he referred to as 'happy Holloway', by wearing his prison uniform every year on the anniversary of his conviction.

William Thomas Stead, editor of the *Pall Mall Gazette*, sent to prison for his role in the 'Maiden Tribute of Modern Babylon'.

A letter sent by W. T. Stead in answer to one of his detractors during his imprisonment.

CRIMES OF THEIR TIME

THE NINETEENTH CENTURY brought unprecedented developments in industry, transport and society; with these dramatic changes came new crimes unique to and in many ways impossible before this new age. The growing railway network of the nineteenth century was soon used by fraudsters and confidence tricksters to travel from place to place, committing their crimes and then fleeing when they had achieved their deception or when suspicion fell upon them. The seclusion of railway carriages without corridors also led to a number of opportunistic but often very violent robberies; it was only a matter of time before one of these attacks ended in murder.

On 9 July 1864 Thomas Briggs, a city banker, was attacked and robbed on a train, and his body was thrown from the carriage onto the tracks between Bow and Hackney Wick stations on the North London Railway. Found alive, he was removed to a nearby pub but later died of his wounds. The crime received a great deal of press coverage, and a reward of £300 was offered for information leading to the capture of the murderer. Suspicion fell upon Franz Muller, who when arrested was found with Briggs's gold watch and his hat, which Muller had picked up in error, leaving his own behind in his haste to flee the carriage. Muller was the first person to be executed for a murder on a railway.

Franz Muller, the first man to commit a murder on a railway train.

Another murderer who committed his crime on the railway was Percy Lefroy Mapleton. On 27 June 1881 he attacked, robbed and threw his victim from a train but his case was to prove significant for the advancement of criminal detection. Mapleton had drawn immediate attention on the station where he alighted but he slipped away. A manhunt ensued, led by C. E. Howard Vincent, Director of the CID, who called upon the British press for their assistance. For the first time the description of the wanted person was accompanied by an artist's impression. Published in the *Daily*

Murder in the Railway Train.

Listen to my song, and I will not detain you long,
And then I will tell you of what I've heard.
Of a murder that's been done, by some wicked one,
And the place where it all occurred ;
Between Stepney and Bow they struck the fatal blow,
To resist he tried all in vain,
Murdered by some prigs was poor Mr Briggs
Whilst riding in a railway train.

Muller is accused, at present we cannot refuse
To believe that he is the very one,
But all his actions, you see, have been so very free,
Ever since the murder it was done ;
From his home he never went, but such a happy time he spent,
He never looked troubled on the brain,
If he'd been the guilty man, he would have hid all he can,
From the murder in the railway train.

Muller he did state that he was going to emigrate
Long before this dreadful tragedy ;
He often used to talk, about travelling to New York,
In the Victoria, that was going to sea.
Mr. Death, the jeweller, said, he was very much afraid,
He might not know the same man again,
When he heard of the reward, he started out abroad,
About the murder in the railway train.

If it's Muller, we can't deny, on the Cabman keep your eye,
Remember what he said the other day,
That Muller a ticket sold for money, which seems so very funny,
When he had no expenses for to pay.
They say his money he took, and his name entered on the book,

Long before this tragedy he came ;
Like Muller's, the Cabman had a hat, and it may be his, perhaps
That was found in the railway train.

Would a murderer have forgot, to have destroyed the jeweller's box,
Or burnt up the sleeve of his coat,
Would he the chain ticket have sold, and himself exposed so bold,
And to all his friends a letter wrote,
Before Muller went away, why did not the cabman say,
And not give him so much start on the main
If the cabman knew—it's very wrong—to keep the secret up so long,
About the murder in the railway train.

When Muller does arrive, we shall not be much surprised,
To hear that that's him on the trial ;
Give him time to repent, though he is not innocent,
To hear the evidence give no denial.
Muller's got the watch, you see, so it proves that he is guilty,
But like Townley don't prove that he's insane
For if it should be him, on the gallows let him swing,
For the murder on the railway train.

Now Muller's caught at last, tho' he's been so very fast,
And on him they found the watch and hat,
Tho' across the ocean he did roam, he had better stayed at home,
And hid himself in some little crack,
Tho' he pleads his innocence, but that is all nonsense,
For they'll hang him as sure as he's a man,
For he got up to his rigs, and murdered Mr. Briggs
While riding in a railway train.

London : Printed for the Vendors.

Broadside verses published at the time of Muller's conviction.

Telegraph, it created enormous public interest, which resulted in erroneous sightings of the wanted man all over the country. Mapleton was traced through detective work rather than being identified from his published image, but the police had found such images were a valuable asset to raise the profile of their investigations, and they are still used to this day.

The proliferation of people earning large amounts of money in the industrial age meant that unprecedented numbers were vulnerable to the ploys of fraudsters. Often coming from the very class they intended to deceive, fraudsters were usually well educated, intelligent, well mannered and, above all, plausible. Many could have succeeded in any number of professions but they were motivated by their own financial problems,

The wanted poster for Percy Lefroy Mapleton – the first to use an artist's impression of a suspect.

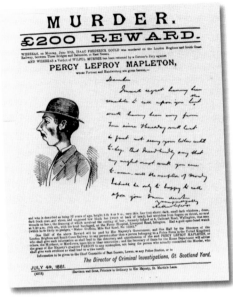

A *Police Gazette* from 1881 containing a number of requests for information about crimes committed on railways.

unrealistic aspirations, addictions such as gambling, high living or women, or purely by greed.

At a petty crime level, 'white collar' embezzlers creamed off money from businesses, sometimes over weeks, months and even years before detection, while others in a moment of weakness stole from a cash box or safe. Prosecution of these criminals varied; some received the full rigour of the law and were given custodial sentences, while others were quietly dismissed to avoid a scandal or bad publicity.

For the more sophisticated or brazen fraudster, shares were always a popular scam; apparently safe investments tempted many of the new middle

John Novitsky, a Russian wanted on warrant for stealing a number of Bonds. Age about 45; height; 5ft 7in.; full beard and moustache fair; hair dark brown, turning grey, slightly curled; dress grey trousers, black coat and waistcoat; ~~took with him~~ Supposed to have been a Russian Officer, and a correspondent for the Moscow Gazette. A Reward of £100. is offered for information leading to this mans apprehension.

Metropolitan Police London
2nd September 1872.

Above and above left: A photograph of John Novitsky, wanted on warrant for stealing bonds. On the back the picture was supplied by the Metropolitan Police with a description of the man to a local printer to create a poster for public display and circulation, September 1882.

class, and even those with 'old money', to entrust their capital to unscrupulous companies, and to speculate in enterprises ranging from gold mines in far-flung corners of the world to the railways being constructed across Britain during the 'mania' of the 1840s. Auditing of accounts was minimal, and the performance of companies could easily be manipulated to deceive investors, who might then lose heavily when the company collapsed. Others set up completely fraudulent 'fronts' for apparently viable investment opportunities and simply absconded with the money.

There were also numerous incidents of fraud whereby criminals impersonated military officers, policemen or gentry with the intent to deceive; the most notorious of these was Arthur Orton (also known as Thomas Castro), remembered as the 'Tichborne Claimant'. The son of a Wapping butcher, Orton had been bankrupted in England, emigrated to Australia and emerged again in 1863 when the dowager Lady Tichborne placed appeals in newspapers worldwide seeking news of her lost son. Orton boldly claimed to be the missing heir, Lady Tichborne was utterly convinced by the deception and Orton laid claim to the family estates. Relatives and friends of the Tichbornes remained unconvinced and Orton was taken to court.

The resulting case was the longest fought in British judicial history, spanning 1,025 days, and legal costs amounted to £200,000 (£10 million at modern values). Orton was convicted on two counts of perjury on 28 February 1874 and sentenced to fourteen years' hard labour. Released on ticket-of-leave in 1884, he joined a circus and died in obscurity and poverty.

The upright society so keen to extol Victorian values provided a façade for a hideous business that became known as 'baby farming'. If an unmarried girl became pregnant, one option to deal with the situation was to scan the newspapers for an advertisement such as this:

ADOPTION: A good home, with a mother's love and care, is offered to a respectable person, wishing her child to be entirely adopted. Premium £5 which includes everything. Apply to Mrs – by letter only…

Arthur Orton, the 'Tichborne Claimant'.

After a short exchange of letters, terms would be agreed. The woman who was contacted would have given assurances that the baby would be found an adoptive home with a good family. A meeting would be arranged, cash would be paid and the baby would be handed over, thus removing the 'problem' – out of sight, out of mind. However, despite the dangers of childbearing and the high rate of child mortality, the supply of unwanted children far outweighed the demand, and homes could not be found for all the babies. In a number of cases these unfortunate children were kept in a house and left to die from neglect or from untreated childhood illnesses, but the baby farmers would have to be cunning enough to elude the interest of the police, the inspectors of the newly formed NSPCC or doctors who might become suspicious about the number of infant deaths they had been called to certify. In other instances the poor babies were taken to railway stations some distance away and abandoned, while others were dumped in a dark alley with no regard to the likelihood of their discovery or survival.

A number of women were prosecuted for baby farming in the late nineteenth century, the most notorious of whom was Amelia 'Annie' Elizabeth Dyer, a trained nurse who found a far more lucrative business in baby farming. Dyer moved around the country, using many aliases to avoid detection, but she was finally traced after a baby wrapped in a brown-paper parcel was pulled out of the river at Caversham Lock, Reading. The wrapping still carried Dyer's old address and a witness had spotted her on the towpath with a parcel under her arm. The waters were searched and a further six

bodies were found. Dyer had been carrying on her trade for about twenty years and it has been estimated that the number of babies entrusted to her care amounted to dozens, perhaps over fifty. Many of their tiny bodies were never found, but, chillingly, when Mrs Dyer was asked about the identification of her victims she replied: 'You'll know mine by the tape around their necks.' Mrs Dyer was executed on 10 June 1896.

Above: Police recover an abandoned baby, as illustrated in *On and Off Duty*, 1887.

Left: Mrs Amelia 'Annie' Dyer.

REFORM

LIKE MANY SOCIAL ILLS during the Victorian period, crime and criminality were treated by most 'decent' people with utter disdain. Any action to alleviate the causes of criminality or the deprivation that led to crime was conducted predominantly by religious organisations such as the Quakers, the Salvation Army or the Church of England, or by individual benefactors associated with them. Christian magazines such as *The Quiver* or *Home Words* also reflected this trend with illustrated stories of how their work and guidance led 'lost souls' of the poor away from the slippery path of drink, debauchery and crime to salvation in the Lord. Regrettably, many of those on the receiving end of such outreach work were grateful for the free food and handouts but saw anything more as meddlesome interference in their lives. In some areas, when the Salvation Army marched through the street with their bands playing, crowds came out to mock and pelted then with rubbish; hence the bonnets worn by the sisters of the Salvation Army in those early years were far more for protection than to act as a uniform.

The reform of those who had been convicted and sent to prison was handled in two ways. Those tried, found guilty and imprisoned for their crimes in a locally administered county, city or borough prison on a sentence of a month or less would be exposed to what was intended to be a short sharp shock of 'hard bed and hard labour', both to punish the prisoner and to provide a deterrence from future acts. Those sent down for longer periods, especially convicts sent to national prisons such as Millbank or Pentonville, would be subjected to attempts to reform them based around a daily routine of religious observance, education and labour. When released on 'ticket-of-leave', the ex-convict would have to report to a police station regularly for a set time, but any form of probation work was limited and was provided by such organisations as the Church of England Temperance Society, which appointed missionaries to the London Police Courts, or the Discharged Prisoners Aid Society. This system was replaced in 1907, when the supervision of discharged offenders was made statutory, and courts were able to appoint and employ probation officers.

Opposite:
The path to salvation as depicted in *In Darkest England and the Way Out* by Salvation Army founder General William Booth (1890).

One of the Salvation Army 'slum saviours', who reached out to the poor in the East End of London, c. 1888.

The Salvation Army pelted on the streets as they marched by in the 1890s.

The most proactive measures for the reform of convicted felons in the nineteenth century were those aimed at child criminals. Succour for wayward children was well publicised in newspapers and Christian publications and fitted well with Victorian values. Christian societies working within the prison system were keen to emphasise the notion that the criminal child really could be reformed before criminality became ingrained. Child criminality also often featured in popular literature

in the nineteenth century. When he was a young man, Charles Dickens had seen gangs of street children recruited, trained and directed to commit criminal acts by adults, and he saw prisons first-hand when he visited his father, who was imprisoned for debt in the Marshalsea Prison. Dickens made the life of one young boy drawn into crime through no fault of his own the central theme of his book *Oliver Twist* (1838); such was the popularity of this work that the powerful imagery invoking sympathy for Oliver and hatred for such characters as Fagin lingered throughout the nineteenth century.

Julia Ann Crumpling, aged seven, served seven days' hard labour in Oxford Gaol for stealing a pram in 1870.

With the creation of effective police forces in urban areas, and slum clearance, most criminal gangs of children led by adults faded away by the 1860s but child crime still existed, especially among children whose families were so poor they could not afford to eat, or those children on the streets with no family at all. Child crime was often extremely petty, with such acts as stealing something to sell, stealing money or stealing things to eat being commonplace in court records. Up to the late nineteenth century, courts would sentence first-time child offenders, some as young as ten, to their own 'short sharp shock' of being whipped or birched, followed by three to ten days in prison with hard labour.

Imprisonment of children in adult prisons was unsuitable and could turn children into even harder and more skilled criminals; this

Arthur Broderick, aged twelve, served one month at Wisbech Prison for stealing goods to the value of 2s in 1872.

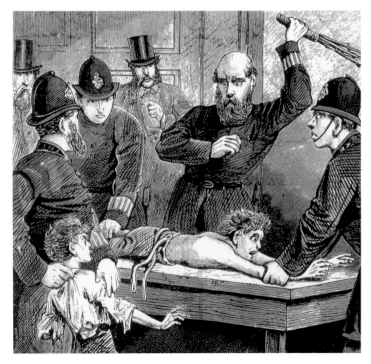

Birching a child offender, 1877.

situation was addressed by the Youthful Offenders Act (1854), whereby children under sixteen found guilty of crimes could be sent to prison for a maximum of fourteen days; they would then be removed to reformatory schools for between two and five years. The results of this system showed children benefiting from a routine, being given an education and a sense of responsibility. Punishment was an essential part of the strict regime, which included freezing cold baths, military-style drills and hard physical labour. The scheme also paved the way for the Industrial Schools Act (1866), which created establishments for orphans, children of convicted criminals and refractory children, who would be subject to a strictly instructed basic education, and training in industrial and agricultural processes. Despite these best efforts, juveniles were still being sent to prisons until the introduction in 1900 of the Borstal system of reformatory prisons for young offenders guilty of serious or repeat offences.

Alice Fanny Elkins, aged thirteen, convicted of larceny at Farnham in 1873 and sentenced to one month in prison and five years at the Surrey Girls Reformatory.

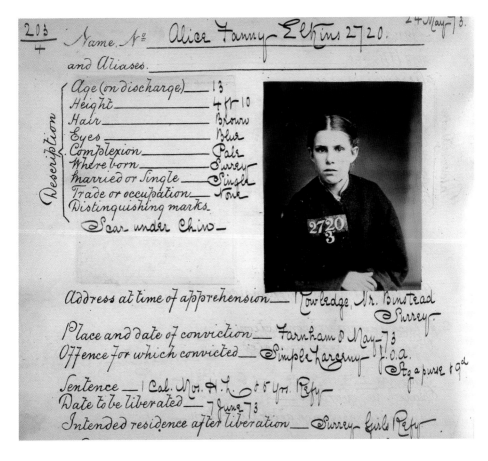

THE
LIFE and EXECUTION
OF
James Blomfield Rush,
For the MURDERS at Stanfield Hall, on the

Bodies of ISAAC JERMY and

JERMY JERMY, his son,

Who was Executed on the Castle Hill, on Saturday last, in April, 1849.

James Blomfield Rush, is the natural son of the daughter of a farmer, near Wymondham, by a farmer residing near the parish in or near which she lived, to whom she was engaged. From some cause the engagement was broken off, and an action was brought by her for breach of promise of marriage, and heavy damages obtained. Mr. Rush, of Aylsham, not long afterwards married the prisoner's mother. From this year until 1834, Rush's father occupied a farm at Felmingham, the property of the late Rev. George Preston, and subsequently of the late Mr. Jermy, where he died, his death having been attended by somewhat extraordinary circumstances. He was found dead in his kitchen in the day time, with a shot wound behind his ear, a discharged gun lying near him. Several reports were spread respecting this affair, and amongst them, one that a number of persons had been summoned to the house by the son, and when the Coroner arrived, he found his jury as it were ready to his hand. The verdict was Felo-de-se.

The prisoner was brought up by his mother's husband, and put to school with Mr. Nunn, at Eye, in Suffolk. In 1834 he commenced farming at Aylsham, under the Rev. Samuel Pitman, from whom he rented for about four years, 120 acres of land. In 1828 he married the second daughter of a highly respectable yeoman, in the neighbourhood of Aylsham, and took the Wood Dalling hall farm, under W. E. L. Bulwer, Esq. where he expended a considerable sum in improvements. The husband of Rush's mother held a farm at Felmingham, under the Rev. George Preston. Times were very hard for farming, and he often talked of giving up his farms, and he said I should have what part I liked when he did so, but should prefer my taking the whole; in the mean time, one of his tenants at Felmingham would not hold under him any longer; he wished me to take that, he did so, under an agreement for 18 years, from Michaelmas, 1835, at £110 per annum.

He took the Stanfield hall farm for 21 years, at £500 per annum; In 1837 the Rev. George Preston died; Mr. Jermy, his son, the late Recorder, discovered the leases were not legally made, and this was the beginning of disputes between Mr. Rush and Mr. Jermy.

At the letter part of his occupation of Wood Dalling Hall Farm, Rush commenced and continued the business of valuer and auctioneer, in which he met with some success,

The Potash farm, which was the property of Mr. Calver, was for sale, and as it lies between the Stanfield Hall and Hethel properties of Mr. Jermy, that gentleman had a wish to possess it, as it would have made the property a compact

whole. Rush consulted Mr. Jermy about its purchase, and the latter deputed him to buy it at a certain sum. However, the estate was run up to a higher sum than Mr. Jermy had directed Rush to bid, and Rush bought it for himself. The price was about 130*l*. above Mr. Jermy's bid. Rush informed Mr. Jermy, that although he (Rush) had purchased it, he did not possess the means to pay for it, and requested Mr. Jermy to pay for it, and requested Mr. Jermy to lend him the sum he required on mortgage, 3500*l*. was advanced for which interest was to be paid. After this two more sums were advanced, making 5000*l*, which was not to be called in until ten years after. This term expired two days after the murder.

The daughter of the prisoner, whose decease was confidently reported on saturday, had an interview with he father; she and the rest of the family are as well as under these melancholy circumstances can be expected. Miss Rush, and the younger branches of the family are still at Felmingham; with the exception of one son, who with his eldest brother, Mr. James Rush, is at Potash. The prisoner has nine children.

THE EXECUTION.

This morning the above unhappy culprit paid the forfeit of his life to the offended laws of his country. No execution of late years has attracted so large an assemblage of spectators, some thousands being present. About nine o'clock he took some refreshment, and shortly afterwards the sheriff arrived at the castle, and immediately proceeded to the condemned cell. The usual melancholy preparations having been completed, Rush was brought to the room where he was to be pinioned. He appeared to be quite calm and collected, and walked with a firm step. The melancholy procession then proceeded towards the scaffold, which he mounted without any assistance, and in less than a minute the drop fell, and the wretched malefactor was launched into eternity,

---

O Lord ! receive my sinful soul, have mercy on my guilt;
The blood of Christ have made me whole, for me that blood was spilt

All you that do around me stand, may this a warning be;
Unto the word of God attend, and shun bad company.

You see me here a wretched man, but short will be my stay;
Yet on my Saviour I'll depend, to wash my sins away.

Pray for my soul, good people all, and pity my sad fate;
A moment hence the drop will fall, I have not long to wait.

And may the blood of Jesus Christ, atonement for me make;
On his dear name my comfort rest, he died for sinners' sake.

INFAMOUS MURDERS

T HE FIRST crimes to capture the public's imagination during Queen Victoria's reign were the murders committed by James Blomfield Rush at Stanfield Hall near Wymondham in Norfolk on 28 November 1848. The crime was the culmination of a tangled web of avarice, and its many twists and turns made good copy for the newspapers and held the public's imagination as each new revelation was made.

Rush was a farmer with pretensions of being a country squire but he had a long record of dubious deals and financial problems and was always trying to find legal loopholes to avoid paying his debts or to escape his financial commitments. He also failed to defend suits brought against him for seduction and bastardy by more than one complainant. Rush was to meet his match in Isaac Jermy, the Recorder of Norwich, who knew the law and finance and was not afraid to use them to his advantage.

The mortgage from Isaac Jermy to Rush for his home, Potash Farm, was due for settlement on 30 November 1848, but Rush had no means to pay it. On the night of 28 November 1848 Rush walked the short distance from Potash Farm to Stanfield Hall, where he disguised himself with a mask, wig and whiskers and hid in the shrubbery. When Isaac Jermy stepped out from the hall to take in the evening air after dinner Rush shot him at almost point-blank range. The masked assassin then strode into the building, where he shot dead Jermy's son in the staircase hall and wounded others as they fled upstairs. Despite his disguise, the bulk and gait of Rush were unmistakable and he was soon under arrest. Tried at the Norfolk Assizes in March 1849, Rush arrogantly turned down offers of legal counsel, opting to defend himself. He was often belligerent and attempted to intimidate the prosecution witnesses. When Rush presented his defence, he spoke for fourteen hours. His five witnesses were hardly worthwhile, even damning; among them was Maria Blanchflower, a nurse at Stanfield Hall. She stated she had seen the disguised murderer but did not recognise the figure as Rush, despite having run past within a few feet of him. Rush asked 'Did you pass me quickly' – an unfortunate slip of the tongue, especially in open court.

Opposite:
One of many broadsides composed upon the execution of James Rush, the Stanfield Hall murderer.

Stanfield Hall
near Wymondham,
Norfolk, scene
of the infamous
murders on 28
November 1848.

After a deliberation of just ten minutes, the jury returned a verdict of guilty. Rush was sentenced to death and executed by William Calcraft before a massive crowd at Norwich Castle on 21 April 1849.

Books and broadsides recounting every dramatic and lurid detail of the Stanfield Hall murders sold in unprecedented numbers: the broadside of 'Sorrowful Lamentations' of the murderer sold 2.5 million copies across the

A rare engraving
of James Rush,
sketched from life
while in the dock
at Norfolk Assizes,
1849.

country. Columns, pages and whole supplements were given over to the case in both local and national papers, and Queen Victoria was recorded as taking a personal interest. James Rush was the classic villain of Victorian melodrama, not only in build and dress, but also in his behaviour, manners, morals and the sinister schemes that were exposed at his trial. His wax image, 'taken from life at Norwich', was the star attraction in Madame Tussaud's Chamber of Horrors in 1849. Visitors were recorded as looking into his cold, glassy eyes 'with the most painful interest'. The notoriety of James Blomfield Rush ensured that his figure was on display in the Chamber for over 120 years.

Another face that graced the Chamber of Horrors for many years was that of Dr William Palmer, the 'Rugeley Poisoner'. Working from his surgery in his home

Ticket of admission granted by the Sheriff for a dockside seat in the packed courtroom during the trial of James Rush at the Norfolk Assizes.

town of Rugeley in Staffordshire, Palmer earned a reasonable living but not enough to support his gambling habit; he was often in debt and his situation became more serious as the years went by. A number of suspicious deaths occurred around Palmer, including those of a work colleague, his mother-in-law, five of his children and his wife, whom he had insured for the considerable sum of £13,000. He also insured his wife's brother, who, however, died too soon after the policy was taken out, so the insurance company refused to pay. Child mortality and early deaths were accepted features of life in the nineteenth century and epidemic diseases were rife at the time, so these deaths did not attract particular suspicion.

It was only after Palmer attended the Shrewsbury Handicap Stakes in November 1855 that suspicion fell upon him. Palmer lost heavily but his friend John Cook, who had accompanied him to the races, had done very well. A few days later Cook fell ill and died. At the ensuing inquest the jury returned a verdict of 'wilful murder'. Suspicions of foul play were aroused when Palmer attempted to bribe several people involved with the coroner's inquest, and with the discovery that Palmer had purchased strychnine shortly before Cook's death. Palmer was arrested. The bodies of his wife and her brother were exhumed and re-examined but the findings were inconclusive. It was considered that Palmer would not face an unbiased jury in Staffordshire and so he was tried at the Old Bailey. Found guilty of the murder of John Cook, he was returned to Stafford Prison for execution. Palmer was hanged in front of a crowd of thirty thousand on 14 June 1856. As he stepped onto the gallows, Palmer is said to have looked at the trapdoor and exclaimed: 'Are you sure it's safe?' His mother always believed her son innocent and after his execution commented: 'They have hanged my saintly Billy.'

The nineteenth century is notable for the number of doctors who became infamous murderers. Palmer was the first, but others include Dr Edward William Pritchard, an English doctor working in Glasgow. Convicted of murdering both his wife and his mother-in-law by poisoning,

The Life and Career of William Palmer (1856), a typical nineteenth-century publication produced in the wake of a notorious murder case.

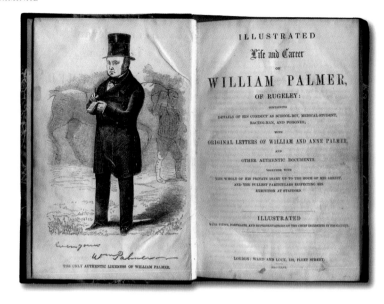

ILLUSTRATED

Life and Career

OF

WILLIAM PALMER,

OF RUGELEY:

CONTAINING

DETAILS OF HIS CONDUCT AS SCHOOL-BOY, MEDICAL-STUDENT, RACING-MAN, AND POISONER;

WITH

ORIGINAL LETTERS OF WILLIAM AND ANNE PALMER,

AND

OTHER AUTHENTIC DOCUMENTS.

TOGETHER WITH

THE WHOLE OF HIS PRIVATE DIARY UP TO THE HOUR OF HIS ARREST, AND THE FULLEST PARTICULARS RESPECTING HIS EXECUTION AT STAFFORD.

ILLUSTRATED

WITH VIEWS, PORTRAITS, AND REPRESENTATIONS OF THE CHIEF INCIDENTS IN THE CAREER.

LONDON: WARD AND LOCK, 158, FLEET STREET.

THE ONLY AUTHENTIC LIKENESS OF WILLIAM PALMER.

Dr George Henry Lamson, the accused at the centre of the 'Wimbledon Mystery', fills the cover of *The Penny Illustrated Paper*, 7 January 1882.

THE PENNY ILLUSTRATED PAPER AND ILLUSTRATED TIMES

THE WIMBLEDON MYSTERY.

Dr G.H. LAMSON.

THE WIMBLEDON MYSTERY: THE PRISONER ACCUSED OF MURDER BY POISON.

he was executed on 28 July 1865. Then there was Dr George Henry Lamson, an intelligent and adventurous young man who seemed to have a promising career ahead of him after qualifying as a doctor in 1874. However, his addiction to morphine lost him his practice and caused him financial difficulties to the extent that he lived by passing false cheques. Lamson stood to inherit over £700, through his wife's interest, if his young disabled nephew Percy were to die. Lamson began poisoning his nephew during a family holiday and continued when the boy returned to Blenheim Special School at Wimbledon. Percy died after a visit from his uncle during which he gave the lad a slice of Dundee cake. An alkaloid poison was detected in the boy's stomach during the postmortem, and a raisin removed from the stomach was tested and found to contain aconite. Lamson was soon under arrest. His trial lasted six days; the jury had no doubt of his guilt, reaching a verdict after just thirty minutes. Lamson was executed at Wandsworth Prison on 28 April 1882.

Dr Thomas Neill Cream was a serial killer. Born in Glasgow in 1850, Cream qualified in medicine in Canada and practised in Britain, the

United States and Canada, fleeing each country whenever he was suspected of illegal medical practices such as abortions, and when suspicion fell upon him for his connection with the deaths of women by poisoning. Convicted in 1881 of administering poison to Daniel Stott, his mistress's husband, he was released with full remission after serving ten years of a 'life' sentence in Joliet Penitentiary, Illinois. A few days after Cream's arrival back in England, he was up to his old tricks, convincing prostitutes to take drink with 'white stuff' in it, or tablets for supposed medicinal purposes. They died in agony a short time later. He fled back to the United States but returned to London in 1892 and convinced both Emma Shrivell and her companion Alice Marsh to sample his deadly wares. Less than an hour later, both women were suffering convulsions and were taken to St Thomas's Hospital, but one died on the way, the other a short while after arrival. Cream produced posters and letters making accusations to increase his self-importance by demonstrating his knowledge of these crimes. He was soon under arrest, after a prostitute to whom he had offered tablets came forward; she had palmed them away because 'she didn't like the look of them'. His trial was little more than a formality. He was found guilty and sentenced to death. On 15 November 1892, according to Billington, the executioner, just after he had adjusted the hood and noose, as he was pushing the lever Cream piped up with his last deluded statement, 'I'm Jack the…', but the gallows trapdoors fell open and silenced him forever.

Dr Thomas Neill Cream.

Another melodramatic crime was revealed on 11 September 1875 when the dismembered body of a woman, wrapped in two parcels of American cloth, was discovered after police were alerted to a hansom cab on Borough High Street. Inside was Whitechapel Pavilion chorus girl Violet Dash, who had been offered a ride by local businessman Henry Wainwright.

Miss Dash was soon found to have no connection with the horrific discovery and was released, but Wainwright was detained. Enquiries soon revealed that Wainwright, a seemingly respectable family man, had a second family living between his home and his brush warehouse. Here he had lived with Harriet Lane and their two children as Mr and Mrs King. Encountering financial difficulties, Wainwright had cut Harriet's allowance, moved her to cheaper accommodation and sent the children to stay with friends.

The discovery of the dismembered remains of Harriet Lane, sensationalised by the *Illustrated Police News*.

Below right: Henry Wainwright, businessman, pillar of the community, and murderer.

Below: One of Henry Wainwright's billheads, with a later cutting about the case affixed to it.

Harriet went to Wainwright's warehouse to complain, and in the altercation that developed Wainwright shot Harriet and hid her body on the premises.

When bankruptcy forced Wainwright out of his warehouse, the body had to be moved and his brother Thomas assisted with the dismemberment and the packaging. An employee, Alfred Stokes, was suspicious about the packages and raised the alarm. Thomas Wainwright was given seven years' hard labour for his complicity, but Henry was found guilty of murder and sentenced to death. As Wainwright approached the Newgate gallows on 21 December 1885 he called out to those assembled: 'Come to see a man die, have you, you curs?'

Kate Webster was an Irish conwoman working as cook and general servant to a widow, Mrs Julia Martha Thomas, at 2 Mayfield Park Villas, Park Road, Richmond, in January 1879. Mrs Thomas had a reputation as a harsh employer and found it difficult to retain staff because of this. After greatly increasing Webster's workload and finding fault with her work, Mrs Thomas gave notice to her servant. On the Sunday before she was to leave, Webster and Thomas argued. From the early hours of the following morning the sounds of washing and brushing were heard coming from the villa. The washing was hung out, and all seemed normal except for an unusual smell emanating from something cooking in the kitchen. On 5 March 1879 a trunk full of human flesh was washed up by the Thames, a human foot was found in a dunghill, and when Webster started selling Mrs Thomas's clothes awkward questions about where Mrs Thomas was began to be asked. Police investigations found many clues at the villa. Mrs Thomas had been cut up, boiled and burnt on the kitchen and copper grates. Webster had fled to Ireland but was traced, tried, found guilty and executed on 29 July 1879.

Hangman William Marwood draws the cap over Kate Webster's head at her execution at Wandsworth Prison on 29 July 1879.

Adelaide Bartlett at the time of her trial.

Florence 'Florie' Maybrick.

Anyone who employed staff would have shuddered when reading of this case, but one can only wonder how those who had bought the gallipots of meat dripping hawked by Webster felt when they heard how she had dealt with her mistress.

A case that drew national interest was the death of Edwin Bartlett in January 1886. The postmortem revealed that Edwin had been killed by a large dose of chloroform, found in his stomach. The so-called 'Pimlico Mystery' was to become infamous, and the revelations of the illicit relationship between Bartlett's wife Adelaide and her tutor, the Reverend George Dyson, scandalised Victorian society. Beyond the scandal, the case hinged on how the chloroform had been administered. If such a chemical had been given to Edwin Bartlett by force or deception, it would have left his throat and digestive passages burnt and inflamed by the chemical on its way to his stomach. There was no evidence of this; the chemical was found only in his stomach. With no evidence to show how or by whom the chloroform was administered, Adelaide Bartlett was found not guilty. Sir James Paget commented after the verdict: 'Mrs Bartlett was no doubt properly acquitted. But now it is to be hoped that, in the interests of science, she will tell us how she did it!'

One of the most sensational trials of a woman in the late nineteenth century was that of Florence 'Florie' Maybrick. A pretty American from a good family, she married James Maybrick, an English cotton broker twenty-three years her senior, in 1881. They made their home at Battlecrease House in the Liverpool suburb of Aigburth. James Maybrick was not easy to live with: he was known to take concoctions of drugs and maintained a number of mistresses, one of whom bore him five children. The disenchanted Florie took to having a few clandestine liaisons of her own, including a dalliance with her husband's brother Edwin. Her affair with a local businessman, Alfred Brierley, came to the attention of James and, after a violent row during which he assaulted Florie, Maybrick demanded a divorce.

In April 1889 Florie bought flypapers that she knew contained arsenic and soaked them in a bowl of water to obtain the poison for cosmetic use. On 27 April 1889 James was taken ill; the doctor was called and he was treated for acute dyspepsia, but his condition declined and he died on 11 May 1889. Suspicious of the cause of death, Maybrick's brothers requested James's body be examined and traces of arsenic were detected, though not enough to prove fatal. Florie was arrested and tried for murder at the Liverpool

Assizes in July 1889. The evidence against her was flimsy; there was no way of proving Florie had administered the arsenic to James, but it seems her private affairs drew condemnation and she was found guilty more for her lack of morals than by direct evidence of murder. Florie was sentenced to death but was reprieved in favour of penal servitude. Her case became a *cause célèbre* but she was released only after serving fourteen years, in January 1904. Florie returned to the United States and died in poverty in 1941. Among her few remaining possessions a tatty family Bible was discovered. Pressed between its yellowed pages was a scrap of paper which had written upon it, in faded ink, the directions for soaking flypapers for use as a beauty treatment.

A late-nineteenth-century wrapper for flypapers containing arsenic.

Mrs Mary Eleanor Wheeler, aged twenty-four, is better known as Mrs Pearcey, from a carpenter with whom she had lived but never married. For two years she resided at 2 Priory Street, Kentish Town, London, and had among her love interests Frank Hogg, a furniture remover. Hogg also had a liaison with Phoebe Styles and married her when she became pregnant, but Frank carried on seeing Mrs Pearcey and employed her in the marital

The tragic story of Florence Maybrick as depicted in the *Illustrated Police News*.

The murderess Mrs Mary Eleanor Wheeler, better known as Mrs Pearcey.

home to nurse his wife and the baby, also called Phoebe. On 24 October 1890 Mrs Pearcey invited Mrs Hogg and baby Phoebe around for tea; they were never seen alive again. Later that same evening Mrs Hogg's body was discovered on a building site in Crossfield Street. Her throat had been cut, and the mutilations inflicted on her body were so horrific that rumours spread that she had been a victim of Jack the Ripper. A mile away in Hamilton Terrace, St John's Wood, an empty perambulator was discovered covered in blood. The body of baby Phoebe was found on waste ground

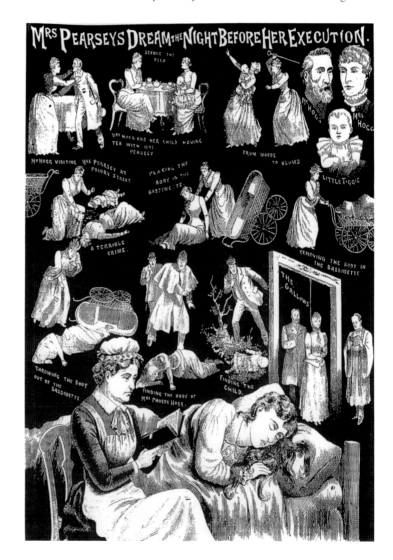

The artist imagines the dream of Mrs Pearcey the night before her execution.

near the Finchley Road a few days later. Frank Hogg had not been too perturbed by the absence of his wife; he thought she had probably gone to visit her sick father, but when he saw newspaper reports about the discovery his concerns were raised, so he sent his sister Clara round to Mrs Pearcey, and the two women went to the mortuary to view the body. Clara recognised her sister-in-law but Pearcey tried to pull her away, insisting it was not her. This strange behaviour caused the police to visit the Pearcey residence. Bloodstains were found on a kitchen knife and poker as well as on her kitchen floor; when asked to explain this she answered vaguely 'Killing mice'. Mrs Pearcey was tried, found guilty and executed on 23 December 1890.

As the nineteenth century drew to a close, a murder fuelled by the age-old motive of jealousy, and symptomatic of Victorian melodrama, occurred on 14 December 1897. One of the leading actors of the day, William Terriss, was stabbed to death at his private entrance to the Adelphi Theatre in London by Richard Archer Prince. Prince, known to acquaintances as 'Mad Archie', was an inveterate letter-writer who sent high-handed missives to theatrical managers who offended him, or fawning letters of commiseration or congratulations to royalty or celebrities, depending on the occasion. He was thought harmless enough by most. During the run of *The Harbour Lights*, in which Prince had a minor role, Terriss took offence to a comment Prince made about him and had Prince dismissed. Terriss, however, sent small sums of money to Prince via the Actors' Benevolent Fund, and continued to try to find him acting engagements. By the end of 1897, however, Prince was destitute and desperate for work, but he had become unemployable. On 13 December Prince attempted to get a complimentary ticket to the vaudeville theatre that adjoined the Adelphi; he was turned down and forcibly ejected. Brooding on this event, Prince was consumed by jealousy of Terriss's success, also blaming the actor for his own miserable situation. The following evening, Prince stepped out of the shadows and carried out his revenge. Convicted of the murder but found insane, Prince spent the rest of his years at Broadmoor criminal lunatic asylum, occasionally putting on concerts with the other inmates until his death there in 1936.

The notable actor William Terriss, murdered at his private entrance to the Adelphi Theatre by Richard Prince on 14 December 1897.

A rare surviving autograph from William Terriss.

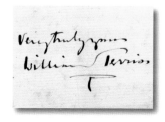

49

THE ILLUSTRATED POLICE NEWS

LAW COURTS AND WEEKLY RECORD

No. 1,284.   SATURDAY, SEPTEMBER 22, 1888.   Price One Penny

"IS HE THE WHITECHAPEL MURDERER?"

READY FOR THE WHITECHAPEL FIEND. WOMEN SECRETLY ARMED.

LATEST DETAILS OF THE WHITECHAPEL MURDERS

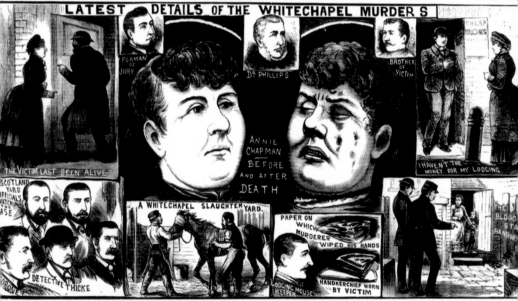

THE VICTIM LAST SEEN ALIVE

FORMAN OF JURY

Dr PHILLIPS

BROTHER OF VICTIM

I HAVEN'T THE MONEY FOR MY LODGING

ANNIE CHAPMAN BEFORE AND AFTER DEATH

SCOTLAND YARD OFFICIALS WATCHING THE CASE

DETECTIVE THICKE

A WHITECHAPEL SLAUGHTER YARD.

LODGING HOUSE KEEPER

PAPER ON WHICH MURDERER WIPED HIS HANDS

HANDKERCHIEF WORN BY VICTIM

EXCITING SCENE IN BOSTOCK AND WOMBWELL'S MENAGERIE

MORE HORRIBLE MYSTERIES.

JACK THE RIPPER

DURING THE AUTUMN of 1888 a series of horrific murders committed in the East End of London alarmed the nation and became all the more grimly fascinating because the murderer was never caught. His sobriquet, however, lives in infamy – Jack the Ripper.

The press in 1888, urban myth and later authors have ascribed numerous murders to this killer, but just five are widely agreed by most crime historians as being victims of Jack the Ripper. The first murder was that of Mary 'Polly' Nicholls (forty-two), whose body was discovered in the early hours of 31 August 1888 on Buck's Row, Whitechapel. The terrible injuries inflicted upon her prompted national and local newspapers to carry lurid accounts of the 'East End horror'.

This horrific and apparently motiveless murder provoked concerns that an insane killer might be at large in the East End of London. Several earlier knife attacks and murders were soon ascribed, mostly by the press, to the person they were now calling the 'Whitechapel Fiend', or 'Leather Apron', because it was believed by many that the killer was a slaughterman. Inspector Frederick Abberline and his team were despatched from Scotland Yard to investigate the murder.

In the early hours of 8 September 1888 the murderer struck again. Annie Chapman (forty-seven) was discovered at the rear of 29 Hanbury Street, Spitalfields. The wounds and mutilation inflicted upon her were even more horrific, and fear grew as the police drew a blank in their hunt for the killer. An unexpected twist to the crime came from the evidence of Divisional-Surgeon Dr George Bagster Phillips at the inquest, when he stated that he believed the work of the murderer 'did show some anatomical knowledge'. This statement rocked society for it implied the murderer was not an ordinary man: the crazed, murdering maniac might be an educated gentleman. In his summing up, the coroner, Wynne Baxter, revealed that he had received a communication from the sub-curator of the Pathological Museum, who some months previously had been visited by an American seeking to procure specimens of uterus and offering to pay £20 for each.

Opposite:
The *Illustrated Police News* coverage of the 'Hanbury Street horror', September 1888.

The slaying of 'Polly' Nicholls, the first acknowledged victim of the murderer who was to become known as Jack the Ripper, fills the cover of *The Penny Illustrated Paper*, 8 September 1888.

The cry of 'Murder in the East End' was often shouted by newsboys in the late nineteenth century.

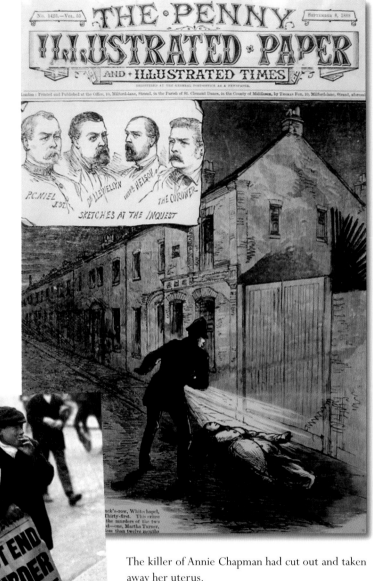

The killer of Annie Chapman had cut out and taken away her uterus.

A letter purporting to come from the killer arrived at the Central News Agency, postmarked 27 September 1888. It taunted the police and threatened more killings, and was signed 'Jack the Ripper'.

PUNCH, OR THE LONDON CHARIVARI.—September 22, 1888.

MURDER

BLIND-MAN'S BUFF.

(As played by the Police.)

"TURN ROUND THREE TIMES,
AND CATCH WHOM YOU MAY!"

The popular concern over the inability of the police to catch the Whitechapel murderer was succinctly summed up by this cartoon published in *Punch* on 22 September 1888.

Postmortem photograph of Annie Chapman.

The Ripper struck again on the night of 30 September. The body of Elizabeth 'Long Liz' Stride (forty-five) was discovered by Louis Diemshutz at 1 a.m. in Dutfield's Yard, beside the International Working Men's Educational Society club building on Berner Street. Only her throat had been cut; it was assumed the killer had been disturbed. Later that night Jack claimed a second victim. Kate Eddowes (forty-three) was discovered in Mitre Square, more vilely mutilated than any previous victim. This night of horror was to become known

The infamous 'Dear Boss' letter that used the sobriquet 'Jack the Ripper' for the first time.

A surgical knife of the type believed to have been used by Jack the Ripper.

as the 'double event' and concluded with a discovery made by PC Alfred Long of H Division in the doorway of 108–19 Wentworth Model Dwellings, Goulston Street. It was a piece of material, torn from Kate's apron, smeared with blood and faeces, and upon which the murderer had wiped his knife and hands. Above the apron fragment, written 'in a good schoolboy hand', was the statement 'The Juwes are the men that will not be blamed for nothing'. There are two schools of thought about this message: one suggests it was purely a coincidence that the rag was cast away by the murderer and just happened to land under these words, while the other proposes that it was a message left by the killer himself. Sir Charles Warren, the Commissioner of the Metropolitan Police, attended the scene in person; no doubt fearing riots and reprisals against the Jewish population in the East End if such an inflammatory statement became popular knowledge, he had the message copied down and, overruling the other officers on the scene, gave the order to 'obliterate the writing at once', rather than wait until there was enough light to photograph it. It was to be a controversial decision that would ultimately contribute to his resignation.

After the 'Jack the Ripper' letter sent to the Central News Agency gained publicity, there was a torrent of letters claiming to know Jack the Ripper, or even to be from him. Some were illustrated with lurid drawings and featured lots of red ink. Among the most disturbing missives was one sent to George Lusk, Chairman of the Whitechapel Vigilance Committee.

THE NEMESIS OF NEGLECT.

" THERE FLOATS A PHANTOM ON THE SLUM'S FOUL AIR,
    SHAPING, TO EYES WHICH HAVE THE GIFT OF SEEING,
INTO THE SPECTRE OF THAT LOATHLY LAIR.
        FACE IT—FOR VAIN IS FLEEING!
    RED-HANDED, RUTHLESS, FURTIVE, UNERECT,
    'TIS MURDEROUS CRIME—THE NEMESIS OF NEGLECT!"

The evocative 'Nemesis of Neglect' cartoon published in *Punch* on 29 September 1888, the day before the 'double event'.

A police notice asking for information, distributed in the immediate aftermath of the Ripper murders on 30 September 1888.

He received a small parcel containing a cardboard box. To Lusk's horror, when he opened the box he found it contained a blood-stained letter and half a human kidney. The kidney was examined by Dr Thomas Openshaw at the London Hospital. Openshaw confirmed that it was a longitudinally divided human kidney. The acting City Police Commissioner, Major Henry Smith, wrote in his memoirs that 2 inches of the renal artery (which averages about 3 inches long) remained in the body

POLICE NOTICE.

TO THE OCCUPIER.

On the mornings of Friday, 31st August, Saturday 8th, and Sunday, 30th September 1888, Women were murdered in or near Whitechapel, supposed by some one residing in the immediate neighbourhood. Should you know of any person to whom suspicion is attached, you are earnestly requested to communicate at once with the nearest Police Station.

Metropolitan Police Office
30th September 1888

Printed by McCorquodale & Co. Limited, "The Armoury," Southwark

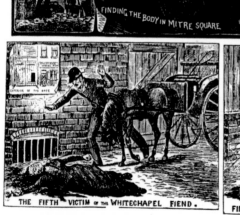

of Kate Eddowes where her kidney had been removed — and 1 inch of artery was all that was attached to the organ sent to Lusk.

The final victim of Jack the Ripper was Mary (Marie Jeanette) Kelly (twenty-five), a common prostitute living and working out of a dingy room, about 12 feet square, at 13 Miller's Court, accessed through a narrow archway off Dorset Street.

On the morning of 9 November 1888 Thomas Bowyer came to chase up Mary Kelly for her rent arrears. After knocking on her door and not receiving an answer, he put his hand through the broken pane and lifted the curtain to see inside. The sight that met Bowyer was beyond normal human imagination. The walls of the room inside were splashed with blood like an abattoir, and on the blood-soaked mattress was an eviscerated human carcass, which had once been the body of Mary Kelly. Those who saw this horror, even seasoned police officers and police surgeons, would never forget what they saw at Miller's Court.

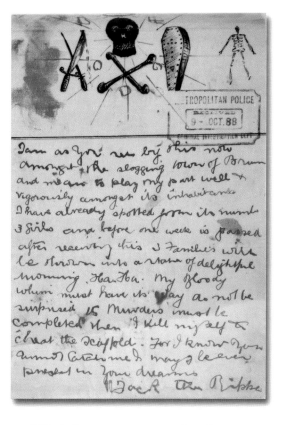

One of many letters sent to the Metropolitan Police claiming to know the identity of the killer, or to be from him, sent in the wake of the 'Dear Boss' letter.

Concern after this event was such that Queen Victoria sent a telegram to the Marquis of Salisbury, the Prime Minister:

> This new most ghastly murder shows the absolute necessity for some very decided action. All courts must be lit, & our detectives improved. They are not what they should be…

The killer known as Jack the Ripper was never brought to justice, but fascination with his crimes continues to this day. Even at the time of the Ripper crimes, chapbooks, lurid exhibitions and the gutter press caused a wider clamour for an insight into the crimes and the 'abyss' of the East End. The Ripper crimes also impacted on the London stage as the American actor Richard Mansfield performed in his acclaimed stage adaptation of Robert Louis Stevenson's *Dr Jekyll and Mr Hyde* at the Lyceum Theatre. Since Stevenson's book was first published in 1886, Victorian sensibilities

Opposite:
The *Illustrated Police News* cover stories of the 'double event' murders of Elizabeth 'Long Liz' Stride and Catherine 'Kate' Eddowes on 30 September 1888.

The cover of *Famous Crimes* reconstructs the horror of Thomas Bowyer after he looked through the broken window at Miller's Court and discovered the eviscerated body of Mary Kelly.

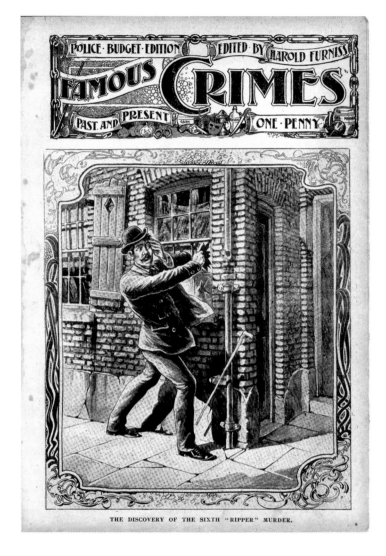

POLICE · BUDGET · EDITION — EDITED BY HAROLD FURNISS

FAMOUS CRIMES

PAST AND PRESENT — ONE · PENNY

THE DISCOVERY OF THE SIXTH "RIPPER" MURDER.

had been outraged by the premise that every human being has a demon imprisoned within them that the right concoctions of chemicals could release on society, to indulge in an orgy of debauchery and malevolence. The consciences of many were troubled by the implication that the Ripper's crimes may have been committed by a gentleman, combined with Mansfield's transformation from the upright Dr Jekyll to hideous Mr Hyde 'in all his blood curdling repulsiveness'. Accusations were made that the play was responsible in some way for the murders (some even suspected

Mansfield himself of being the Ripper); the run of the play was cut short and terminated in its tenth week.

That was, of course, not the last to be heard of Jekyll and Hyde, nor of Jack the Ripper, as the imagery of the swirling fog and the gaslit streets of Victorian London has continued to capture the imagination of successive generations in books, films and on television. Fictional Victorian criminals such as Dickens's Fagin and Bill Sykes are still portrayed, as is Sherlock Holmes, the great detective, but Jack the Ripper endures above all. He has been played by Ivor Novello in *The Lodger* (1927), and the Ripper was amalgamated with the Vampire in such films as *London after Midnight*, starring Lon Chaney (1927). Bram Stoker confirmed he had been influenced in his creation of *Dracula* (1897) by the Ripper murders and the climate of fear during the autumn of terror in 1888. Subsequent fictional investigations of the Ripper

Above: The stalking menace of Jack the Ripper after the Mary Kelly murder epitomised in the *Illustrated Police News*.

Left: In the years after the acknowledged Ripper murders, there were other violent murders in the same neighbourhood, such as that of Frances Coles, who had her throat cut in Swallow Gardens, Whitechapel, on 13 February 1891.

AGNES CAREW MISS CAMERON

Dr JEKYLL & Mr HYDE
THE MURDER OF GENl CAREW

Mr HYDE, I BELIEVE

Dr JEKYLL, Mr Rd MANSFIELD   GABRIEL UTTERSON, Mr SULLIVAN   Mr HYDE, Mr Rd MANSFIELD

Illustrations from Richard Mansfield's performance of *Dr Jeckyll and Mr Hyde* in 1888.

were led by Michael Caine on television and on film by Johnny Depp in *From Hell*. More recently the Ripper's crimes have been imitated fictionally by a copycat killer in the ITV series *Whitechapel*. Nor will that be the last we hear of him. Jack the Ripper's legacy from beyond the grave even extends to the skipping chant of East End children, who proclaim the only thing we know for sure about Jack the Ripper today:

Jack the Ripper's dead,
And lying on his bed.
He cut his throat
With Sunlight soap.
Jack the Ripper's dead.

THE STRAND MAGAZINE

SOUTHAMPTON STREET

359

EDITED By Geo Newnes OFFICES

AN·ILLUSTRATED·MONTHLY·

The Strand Magazine, in which many of the Sherlock Holmes stories were serialised between 1891 and 1927.

William Gillette, one of the first actors to portray Sherlock Holmes, both on stage and in film.

Donald McCormick's *The Identity of Jack the Ripper* (1962): one of hundreds of books published over the years about the crimes of Jack the Ripper, and proposing suspects for the murders.

GREAT PAN

The Identity of
JACK the RIPPER
Donald McCormick

A chilling probe which unmasks history's most gruesome murderer, the Butcher of Whitechapel

A classic
on this classic case SUNDAY TIME
2′6

FURTHER READING

Birkett, Sir Norman (editor). *The New Newgate Calendar*. Folio Society, 1951.

Carter, Michael J. *Peasants and Poachers: A Study in Rural Disorder*. Boydell Press, 1980.

Dell, Simon. *The Victorian Policeman*. Shire, 2004.

Evans, Stewart P., and Skinner, Keith. *The Ultimate Jack the Ripper Sourcebook*. Robinson Publishing, 2002.

Fido, Martin. *The Chronicle of Crime*. Carlton Books, 1993.

Gaute, J. H. H., and Odell, Robin. *The Murderers' Who's Who*. Harrap, 1979.

Gray, Adrian. *Crime and Criminals of Victorian London*. Phillimore, 2006.

Griffiths, Major Arthur. *Mysteries of Police and Crime* (volumes 1–3). Cassell, 1902.

Herber, Mark. *Criminal London*. Phillimore & Co, 2002.

Honeycombe, Gordon. *The Complete Murders of the Black Museum*. Leopard Books, 1995.

Humphrys, John. *Poachers' Tales*. David & Charles, 1991.

Ingram, Arthur. *Trapping and Poaching*. Shire, 1978.

Jones, Steve. *Capital Punishments, Crime and Prison Conditions in Victorian Times*. Wicked Publications, 1992.

Jones, Steve. *The Illustrated Police News*. Wicked Publications, 2002.

Lane, Brian. *The Murder Guide*. Robinson Publishing, 1991.

Lustgarten, Edgar. *A Century of Murderers*. Methuen Publishing, 1975.

Mayhew, Henry. *London Labour and the London Poor: Those That Will Not Work*. Griffin Bohn, 1862.

Paley, Ruth. *Family Skeletons: Exploring the Lives of Our Disreputable Ancestors*. The National Archives, 2005.

Pelham, Camden. *The Chronicles of Crime*. Reeves & Turner, 1886.

Scott, Sir Harold. *The Concise Encyclopedia of Crime and Criminals*. Deutsch 1965.

Shew, E. Spencer. *A Companion to Murder*. Cassell, 1960.

Shew, E. Spencer. *A Second Companion to Murder*. Cassell, 1961.

Storey, Neil R. *A Grim Almanac of Jack the Ripper's London*. Sutton Publishing, 2004.

Storey, Neil R. *London Crime, Death and Debauchery*. Sutton Publishing, 2007.

Storey, Neil R. *Victorian Prisons and Prisoners*. History Press, 2010.

Symons, Julian. *Crime and Detection: An Illustrated History from 1840*. Panther, 1968.

Tobias, J. J. *Nineteenth Century Crime: Prevention and Punishment*. David & Charles, 1972.